**Becoming a ]**

Out on the wastes of the Beacon's windy heather,

That's where the dead men lie.

There, where the cold winds blow forever,

That's where the dead men lie.

That's where the earths strongest sons are keeping,

Endless going; the west wind sweeping,

Feverish weather will never wake their sleeping,

Out where the dead men lie.

T.W

South West London

**Character is higher than intellect... A great soul will be strong to live, as well as to think.**

**Ralph Waldo Emerson**

My eyes were locked on the framed windows of the timber door, staring and waiting to be exposed.

Captured at last.

The building was small, maybe six feet square and I sat, hunched with my back against the wall, curled in amongst some unused boxes and household items that no longer had a place in the home.

The woman came to door of the shed and peered in, slowly she turned the handle and I awaited my eventual fate.

"Don't move" I told myself, and froze.

She slowly made her way inside no more than three feet from me but, so far, the clutter had deceived her and I was temporarily undiscovered.

I stopped breathing with my eyes locked onto her face as she came towards me, an armful of items.

As she placed them by my feet I wondered if she was toying with me. If she had seen me before and knew I was in there hiding like an animal. Maybe it was some kind of sinister trap that I would fall into miserably. Maybe my fate would be worse than I had already imagined.

She turned, humming softly to herself and finally left pulling the thin door closed behind her and made her way back into the house.

I had survived.

After several minutes I tentatively moved out of my position and made my own way out of the shed. Slowly I moved across the garden, eyes fixed on the windows at the back of the house for fear of being caught at the final hurdle, and then swift, with a rush of adrenaline I was over the garden fence and away. Free.

I was fourteen and bunking off school. I hid at my mothers feet in my sisters play shed at the bottom of our garden.

That day I learnt control. I learnt that movement will always betray my position and that, I was in control of my mind and body.

I learnt how to hide and how to be still and calm. I learnt that swift, angry movement is necessary at the right time but control is essential always.

It was a lesson that stayed.

January

Home time

**The loser at the hazard, when the game breaks up, sadder and sorrier lingers on alone, re-plays each throw, and drinks from wisdoms cup.**

**Dante**

I regurgitated a quote I had read a few years before about the first rule of fatherhood was to be present as much as possible and that, if I carried on their path I would be breaking this rule I had set myself many years before.

As I spoke the man sat opposite me, silent and sullen, wearing a grey frown. His large hands and weathered face would deceive a non observant person, they hid his city roots.

I knew him well now. Over many hard weeks and months, he had seen me at my lowest, weakest ebb many times, but he had always remained the same throughout. Quiet, confident and brutal.

It pained me to tell him what I told and eventually my words dried up in the presence of his silent thought, for the first time in all the time I knew this man, I saw a flicker of emotion. Anger, even sadness, but just as quickly, his eyes covered it up.

After a while he lifted his chin from his hands and acknowledged what I had said to him and then we spoke at length.

He asked me if I was sure, if I knew what I was doing was the right thing, but never did he try to persuade me to stay. If I did not want it, then they did not want me. He just wanted to be certain that I knew the implications.

By choosing my own family I had rejected his and it stung him deeply, he wore it in his expression. Perhaps it made him question his own path in life and the family he had once left behind and who had deserted his choice, but I doubt it now.

After all that needed to be said had been, we sat in silence, him in thought and not fond of more words than were necessary and me waiting for approval that would never come.

I glanced up at the dusty, hand etched sign above his desk, "for many are called, but few are chosen", it quoted the bible.

I was one of the chosen ones then, but I had turned it down.

Later that afternoon I left a well known, concrete bunker of a building surrounded by high spiked fences and cameras back into a very ordinary town that rushed by the place without knowing a thing about what went on inside.

The afternoon sun warmed me from the grey interior of the building and I took a moment to turn my face towards it. I would rather be outdoors than in I reminded myself.

I did not look back as I walked away.

Sixteen months before………………..

***What is here, as all that has been written about it,***

***are but words, they will never quite do………………………………***

September

Pre- Selection

**Service life teaches men to live largely on little.**

**T.E. Lawrence**

    As a civilian amongst soldiers I sat in a dusty hall of a gloomy Reserve Army centre waiting to be summoned. I tried to focus on the posters on the wall, or military pamphlets on the stained coffee table but the beat of my heart won out.

Other men were muttering as pairs or in small groups, they all seemed to know each other or knew someone who knew someone else.

Most seemed to have had a life in the army, whether it be regular or reserve and they looked every inch of it. I caught a reflection of myself in the glass of a nearby cabinet. I very nearly stood up and left.

"So how did you come to want to join up with this Regiment?" I was asked by a grey haired man, sat the other side of a leather-bound desk.

His face was weathered but the smile lines and bright eyes somehow defeated the tough exterior. I liked him.

He wore the stripes of a corporal but, out of uniform, I thought he might as well be someone's grandfather. All be it one who could run marathons.

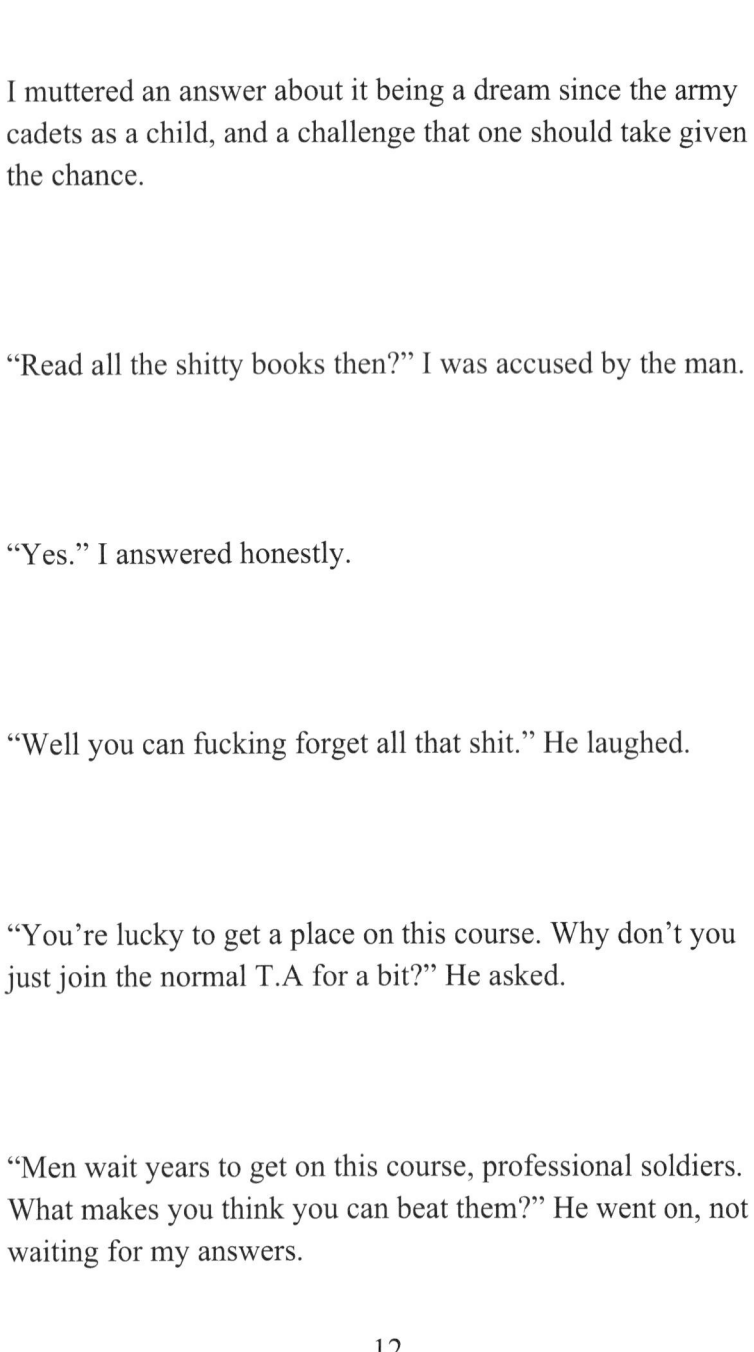

I muttered an answer about it being a dream since the army cadets as a child, and a challenge that one should take given the chance.

"Read all the shitty books then?" I was accused by the man.

"Yes." I answered honestly.

"Well you can fucking forget all that shit." He laughed.

"You're lucky to get a place on this course. Why don't you just join the normal T.A for a bit?" He asked.

"Men wait years to get on this course, professional soldiers. What makes you think you can beat them?" He went on, not waiting for my answers.

This was not going well, I felt he didn't want me already, had seen through my inexperience immediately.

"I'm not sure I can-." I answered honestly again.

I tried to save myself before he sent he home, " – but I'll give it everything I can, and there isn't a man out there-" I gestured towards the busy hall outside, "-who wants it more than me." I protested.

The soldier paused and smiled, he seemed to enjoy my direct answer. For effect he reached into his draw and, the first game began, as he put on his beret. It had seen better days I thought.

"Well an old mutual mate has written on your behalf and if you're good enough for him we'll give you a run out. Fuck off and get your running gear on and send the next cunt in" He said flippantly.

It had begun.

Two hours later my body had already had enough.

We paced around the local park next to the centre and the pain in every part was taking its toll.

One hundred and seventy men had filed out of the centre and we had already lost thirty five. I counted them as they quietly were led away or hobbled off in disgust.

Fit men, fitter than me I thought.

"Up, down" We were instructed.

"Touch ten trees, GO!"

"Press up position, DOWN!"

"Find a fucking partner, what you waiting for wanker?"

"Come on, over take that waster in front of you, he is slowing down."

"Last one back goes again, MOVE."

"No one goes home until I've lost the first forty wasters. Who's it gonna be? GO"

It carried on for thirty more minuets, the last of which are a blur of shouting, pain and dramatic movement.

"Right lads, see you Friday for the first weekend, you've got all this time to recover."

Like cripples we hobbled back to the building. For the only time in the next year the instructors missed their target, they only lost thirty nine men that night.

It was a wet Wednesday evening. I had waited my whole life for this moment.

November

Tests, Tests, Tests

**Courage is doing what you're afraid to do. There can be no courage unless you're scared.**

**Eddie Rikenbacker**

Such detailed, quiet, constant judgement of your character, actions and skills puts pressure on a man and makes him competitive like nothing else or no other organisation in the world can possibly do.

I know this to be true.

Time went by in a rapid haze of extreme physical draining accompanied by mental challenges as the weeks moulded into each other.

Every Wednesday night and weekend I found myself exasperated at why men fell or failed.

Mostly professional soldiers, who didn't give any thought to their movements, or enough action in their preparation to physical and mental tasks set.

Men failed to turn up, or arrived late. They looked for an excuse to be turned away from the unit, or exaggerated injuries.

It wore them.

"Why are you still here, you've outlasted many?" The weathered corporal asked me one drill night as we cleaned weapons.

"Because I think about what's going to happen or will be required in five minuets time rather than now." I answered after some thought.

He laughed and walked away, but I knew he liked the answer.

I was upset at being chosen for a question, I had worked hard to bury myself within the ranks that remained. Never first, never last.

Map reading exams, weapons handling, combat first aid, crushing physical activity, emotional pressure, random tests, odd lessons on non relevant subjects, changeable timetables and strange people saying strange things who I desperately was trying to impress and become one of, became my every day existence.

I would work in the office until five thirty then be doing a half marathon by six followed by lessons until ten.

"Right lads I want you to run ten miles then when you get back, the first person to tell me the average temperature of the North China sea goes home early."

"Here you are boys, a phrase book in Urdu, there will be an exam on Sunday afternoon."

We still had not been told what all this effort would entitle us too. I still knew very little about what these men did after all this, the others on the course seemed to know.

Perhaps I didn't care.

Wednesday was always quickly followed by Friday.

Packing kit at home.

Training every evening after work and before I left in the morning.

Studying for military exams at my desk, the relevant material hidden in my diary so my colleagues could not tell.

Studying ordnance survey maps of Welsh valleys and mountain ranges in my spare time.

Snatching dinner before bed.

Preparing my feet.

Moments with my family.

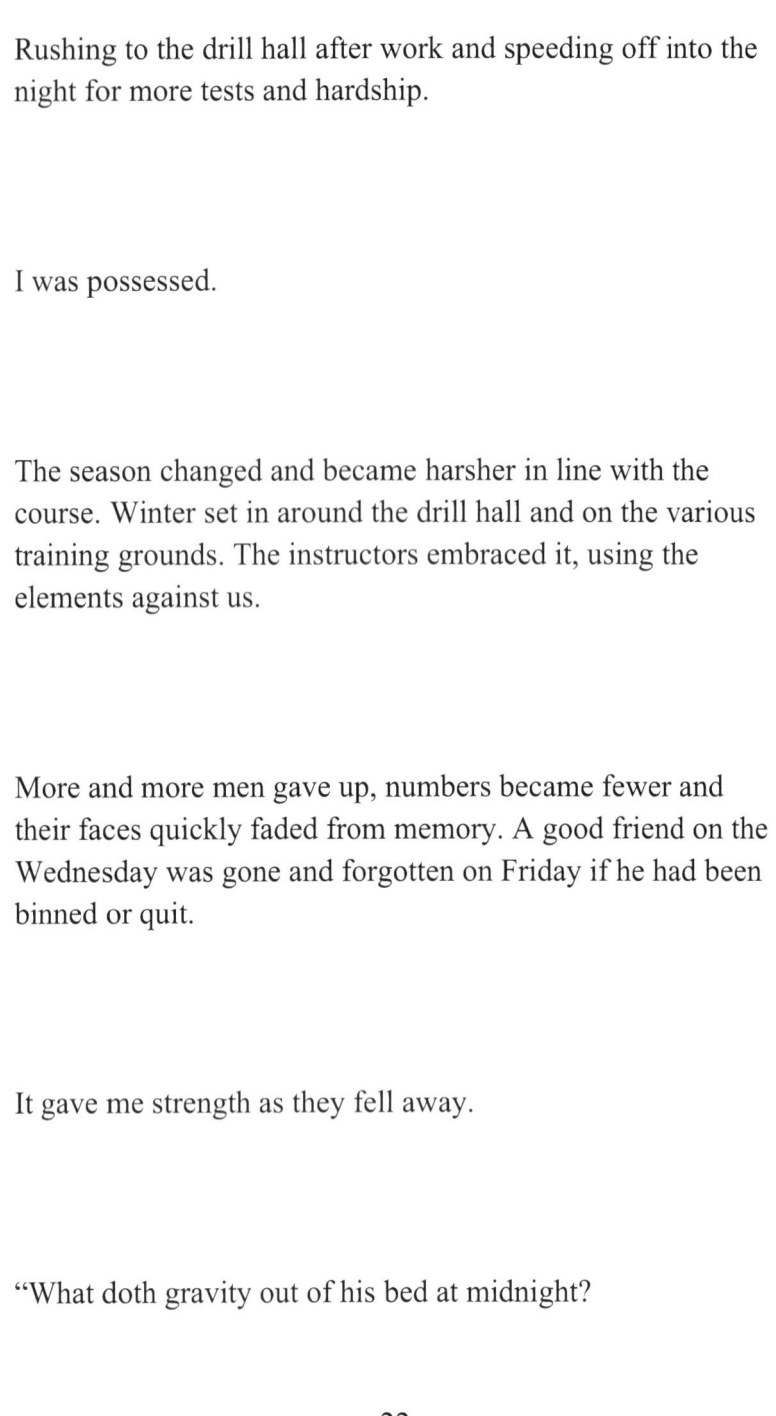

Rushing to the drill hall after work and speeding off into the night for more tests and hardship.

I was possessed.

The season changed and became harsher in line with the course. Winter set in around the drill hall and on the various training grounds. The instructors embraced it, using the elements against us.

More and more men gave up, numbers became fewer and their faces quickly faded from memory. A good friend on the Wednesday was gone and forgotten on Friday if he had been binned or quit.

It gave me strength as they fell away.

"What doth gravity out of his bed at midnight?

Shall I give him his answer?"

Shakespeare

My alarm goes off at five am and I sit on the edge of the bed and instinctively open the curtains of my bedroom to look at the conditions outside. Is it raining or windy? Are there clouds and is it still dark?

These things do not matter really as I know that I will leave my bed and face the elements alone like I do most mornings.

Like a normal person I had given in in the past. Got back into bed and slept through until the day was supposed to begin, however I could not forgive myself on them days. They made me feel weak and angry with myself.

My family sleeps around me and the house is dark. I slip downstairs and drink powered drink for energy.

My filthy boots go on and I step outside into the dark, turning my head torch to red light to give me some light but still not wake me fully.

I find my carefully packed bergan in the dark and force it upon my back awkwardly, always getting my watch caught in the straps and my elbows tied up in the water tubes.

Then I step out, and begin moving.

An hour and a half ahead of me panting and pushing, one foot in front of the other. Alone, with no one asking me to or encouraging me onwards.

Alone, although it is hard I revel in the peace, my own breath and burning legs my ally. I finish this routine before the rest of the worlds wakes, with the peace of sleep and before the chaos of dawn, before the day begins properly.

This is who I am.

December

The Hills

**Now then boys, you have a week or two left. Make the most of it. No preparation can be to thorough for the life that awaits you; relentless; the weakest to the wall.**

**Henry Williamson**

This felt like home to me.

Seventy two men had made it to the hills phase. I already knew them all well by then.

On the Friday night when we arrived at the hills after a long drive up the motorway, the black clouds stood behind them and the rain had already set in.

I remember this first moment clearly, I loved them that night and felt confident. Many days staying at my Grandparents house in the valleys had given me hope as I traipsed across them in my youth, I thought I knew them and had tried them out. I was wrong.

By Sunday afternoon, as we eased back into the transport to fly back down the M4 and home, I was ruined and hated them. I had seen what they could truly do to a man in forty eight short hours.

It was weekend one.

I remember a small, tough man. He had been in a regular infantry regiment for many years and, as civilian life had not suited him, he applied to join the Regiment. He was, quiet and determined and always near the front on most marches, I was sure he would pass.

On the first weekend he noticed my discomfort as my issued helmet flapped awkwardly at my side. All the other men, with their experience, had thought to bring karabiners with them and had strapped them securely onto their webbing.

This man had given me a spare karabiner so I would not be noticed by the staff fiddling with my equipment on the move. It was a kind gesture and saved me from potential reprimand. I still have it to this day.

Two weeks later the small infantryman and myself were paired up on a long night march.

A few hours in, as we went over the crest of the hill he led the way through a sharp blizzard.

A hole in the snow deceived him and he caught his leg in it. The snap of his shin bone sounded like small arms fire and could be heard clearly over the wind.

Unsure of my next move I asked him what to do. His face was screwed up in agony and I could see the bone protruding under his combat trousers.

The next check point was at the crest of a hill, about two kilometres straight up. Knowing that if I left the man he could be lost into the night and succumb to exposure, so I asked my friend to sit on his bergan and, as he quietly moaned and openly cried at the pain, I dragged him to the staffed rendezvous at the summit. His suffering must have been un real.

The tremendous effort carrying both our equipment and a stricken man put me behind on the march and I was allowed to go on alone into the night. Although I came in late nothing was said about my timing, they quietly acknowledged the fact that I had saved his life.

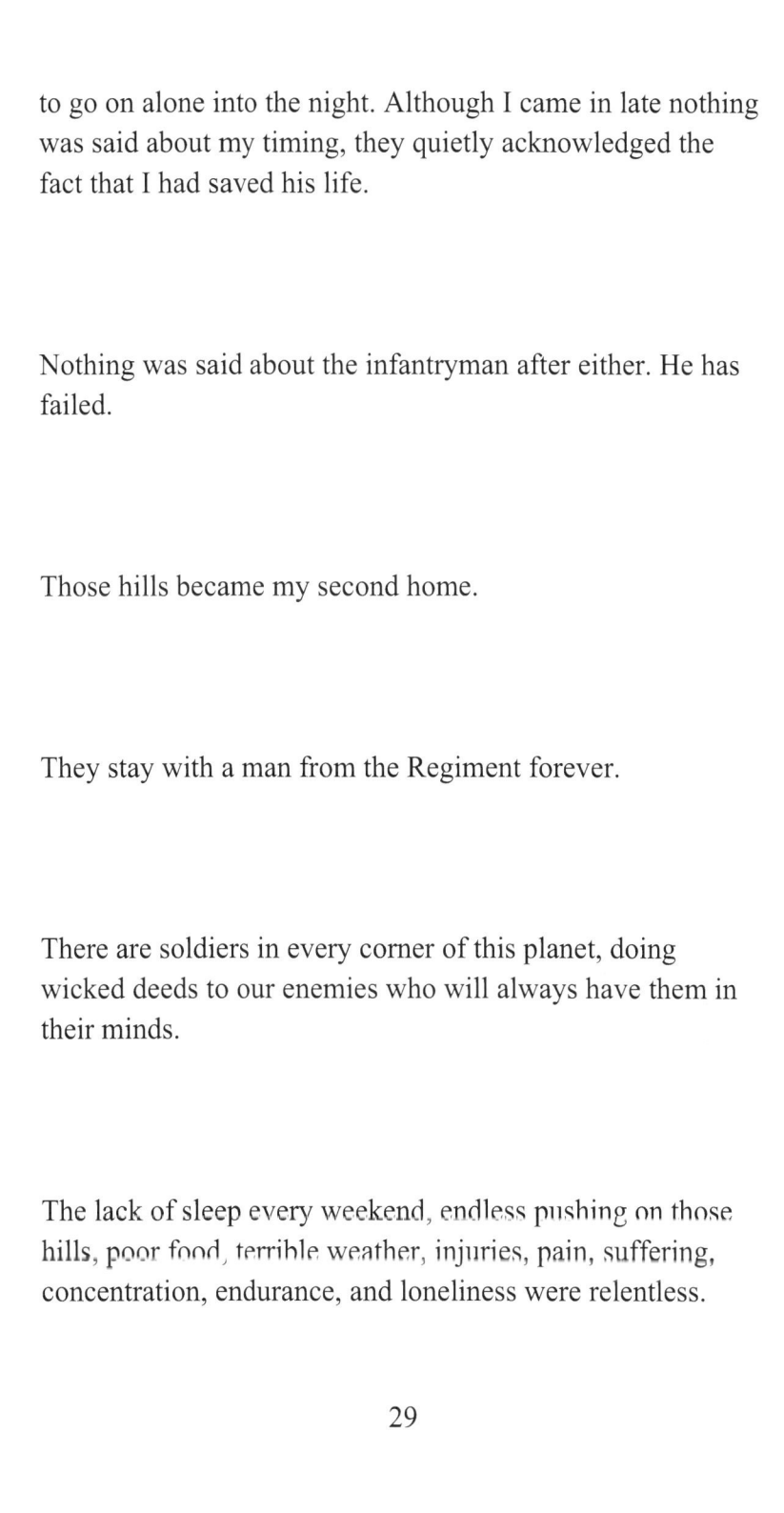

Nothing was said about the infantryman after either. He has failed.

Those hills became my second home.

They stay with a man from the Regiment forever.

There are soldiers in every corner of this planet, doing wicked deeds to our enemies who will always have them in their minds.

The lack of sleep every weekend, endless pushing on those hills, poor food, terrible weather, injuries, pain, suffering, concentration, endurance, and loneliness were relentless.

It went on and, as those who remained got softer, it all got harder.

February

The Main Event

"**I will lift mine eyes unto the hills; from whence cometh my help**"

**Psalm 121**

I looked up and watched the fast moving clouds swiftly shift over the dark green hills and away to an unknown destination far to the East. Silently they screamed away from unknown horrors they had been born to over the dark, unseen Atlantic that dominated the West.

If I could move over the hills as fast as that over the next day and night, fortune would be mine. A fortune that no one could ever buy, and could only be won.

Like camouflaged marathon runners anxiously waiting for the start of the race we squatted, huddled and poised, twitching for the crack of a starter gun that would never fire.

One soldier looked over his shoulder at me and smiled thinly through pursed, white lips. The last remnants of the fading sun shone off of the reflection of his spectacles as it dropped behind a deep, green hill nearby.

The rain finally stopped and the first of the stars began to show, hiding craftily from behind thick clouds.

Dramatic, quiet landscape, falling swiftly into subdued darkness. The world rested while we came alive.

The whiteness of the smiling soldiers' teeth contrasted brilliantly against the grime already smeared across his face, and then, without words, he turned away swiftly, back to the job at hand.

Less than five hours previously I sat at my desk, under the glaring spot lights of a modern office in comfort, and yet, wearing a different kind of uniform.

I discussed the tactics of business with my superiors. But, even then, my mind had wandered to where I am now, thinking about very different tactics, more brutal, more real and, perhaps, more me.

Months of the hardest possible tasks alone had brought me to where I was. I stood amongst a stringy few, and we all knew, not all would make it.

A sudden rustle came from the front of our group, movement from the troops at the front, all keen to carry out the event at hand.

Like an executioners' blade our tall leader raised his hand vertically and dropped it quickly, like trained animals we fell dutifully into our file of falsely armed men carrying archaic rifles from many years ago. Toy soldiers earning the right to make it real.

Away from the vehicles we moved slowly to the base of the first hill, our start point.

The icy cold winds of the Atlantic chased us over the Welsh hills. It danced through our smocks, running its frosty fingers, inherited from far away in Antarctica, over our bodies and under issued protective clothes.

I shivered viciously, cold and eager to start moving over the hills. Movement promised precious warmth, stagnancy was bitter.

"Bearing?" I was asked harshly buy a man in a washed out smock.

I answered by shouting six numbers back at him with false aggression. I knew it is what he wanted to see.

"Which way are you going?" He asked again simply.

With a cold hand I pointed in a direction to the top of the nearest monster and, satisfied he had left enough time and distance from the man in front of me, he finally let me start.

"What you waiting for then?" He asked, a thin smile about his blueing lips.

"Fuck off and get it over with."

I started to climb, cold and alone. However glad of the opportunity to finally stretch my legs after sitting in a cramped vehicle for several hours and at a desk for eight and half hours before that.

Anticipation quickly gave way to lactic burn in my thighs as I swiftly gained height, nearly five stone conspiring wickedly with the forces of nature and gravity, trying desperately to pull me back down towards the centre if the earth.

An estimated forty miles of the greatest country on earth's cruellest mountain range lay before me, I had an unknown time to complete it in and knew only to move as fast as I could.

But I was ready. I knew these hills. I had been here before many times and I knew the tricks, I had to rely on my body to keep going and my mind to switch off. Focus on the bearing, remember the features on the map and keep moving. Injury constantly threatened, pain became numbed.

The first hill was the largest, cold and isolated it stood alone, domineering the others like an angry father standing over its children and casting a frightening shadow.

At its summit I was quickly given six more numbers by a familiar windswept man and, after taking my bearing moved off into the gloom of the vast range in search of this place.

At deeper dusk I found myself in a forestry block and was glad to be out of the wind. The clouds parted briefly and the failing sun shone through the thin trees. It was my favourite time of the day and, for a moment, I forgot my bitter pain from every inch of my body. I will remember this moment forever.

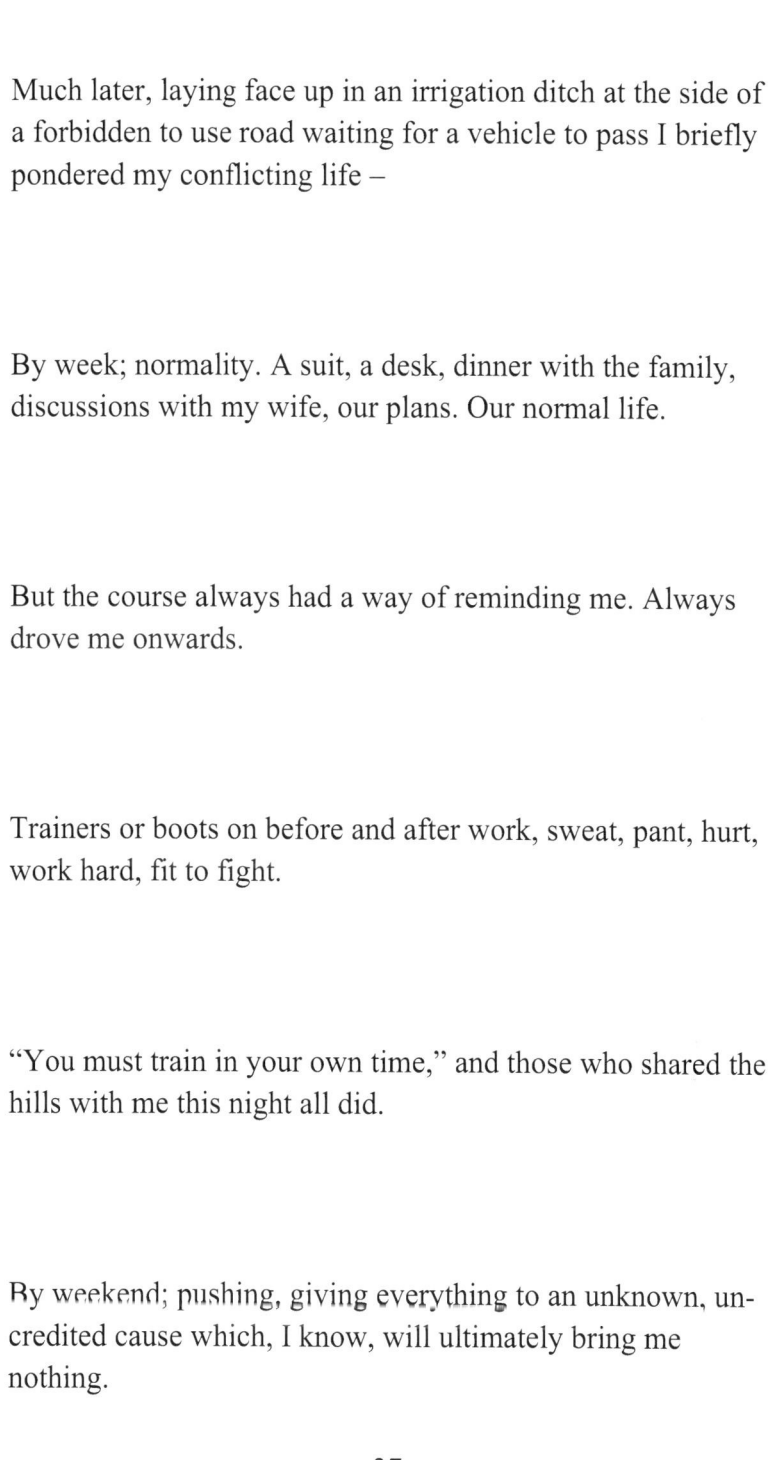

Much later, laying face up in an irrigation ditch at the side of a forbidden to use road waiting for a vehicle to pass I briefly pondered my conflicting life –

By week; normality. A suit, a desk, dinner with the family, discussions with my wife, our plans. Our normal life.

But the course always had a way of reminding me. Always drove me onwards.

Trainers or boots on before and after work, sweat, pant, hurt, work hard, fit to fight.

"You must train in your own time," and those who shared the hills with me this night all did.

By weekend; pushing, giving everything to an unknown, un-credited cause which, I know, will ultimately bring me nothing.

Discretely I had already asked every man that I had joined with including myself, "Why?"

All had given their own answer, own reason but still I found myself waiting for something more valid than the answers they gave, they were my competitors.

Five hours later I moved along a narrow ridge at the top of the bitter mountains. I slipped briefly on a rock that made up part of the old roman road and bashed my right knee badly.

The pain felt good, detracting it briefly from my feet, and aching shoulders I took the opportunity to drop my kit and stand, allowing myself no more than thirty seconds of precious rest.

I stood at the very crest of the monsters surveying the dark land, pondering once again and slipping into alert unconsciousness with exhaustion.

These mountains I had loved as a boy had become my enemy and it saddened me, one day I would come back here, I told myself, and fall in love with them again.

Many hours in, one soldier had stopped in a valley, slumped on his kit he looked sorry. I came across him and, unsure of whether we were being watched, slowed to a brisk walk, my rifle pumping animatedly across my chest. I recognised him from the London squadron, a tall, fit, well spoken, public school type he had spent years as an officer in the regular Calvary.

Exactly the type of thoroughbred man I loved to quietly beat, private education, perhaps a rowing team thrown in, every privilege the world had. He was strong, brave, experienced yet he slumped at my feet.

He was fine, he said. Fearful of moving over uneven ground in the dark and carrying injuries from marches gone by, he risked serious injury, he appealed to me, justifying his failure. He had just had enough.

I understood how he felt. Selfishly I left him where he was. I did not care about his fate. I felt better at my own ability to keep moving and mock courage. Like all them fading faces before, I had beaten him, a waster I determined.

I knew how tough it was. "It's gotta be earned lads", We were continuously told.

"No one will say it's easy, you've gotta want it."

No one will tell you they felt like that on the hills, that kind of talk never drove anyone on in their darkest hour. Whatever did, and whatever made you finish within the strict time came from within. Not big talk or coloured berets. I fucking hate it.

At night I thought of my grandfather and wondered what Welsh hills he had trained on during the war, I slowed to a fast walk and allowed myself to think of him, enjoying the moment. I remembered his stories.

Several miles later the night swallowed me, the hills became black and the weather fiercer., its started to snow in thick clumps. My favourite time on them. I felt safe in the knowledge that no one could see me, watching with scrutiny through a long range telescope or military binoculars.

Clumps of thick moon grass grabbed at my ankles; deep bogs threatened to suck me under, posing disaster for my final hurdle. Evil holes appeared out of the white darkness.

"Stay alert". I told myself aloud, through sleepy whispers, "I'm not home yet"

Standing on the crest of a hill at night I could see large white lights down in the valley. They swept the ground in wide arcs. Vehicles bounced over un even ground.

Unknown to me, a colleague lay, unmoving in a river bed a thousand feet below. The wind had blown him of a cliff face and he lay in the freezing water for over half an hour, still strapped to his equipment.

Fortune followed his bad luck as another recruit stumbled across him before he died of hypothermia and raised the alarm.

He had broken his back and would never walk again. I do not remember his name now.

Many hours later and in and out of conscious thought I wondered for the millionth time why I was here, for what. Why such suffering with such goodness waiting for me at home?

A man who is close to me in my life as I write demands that I use this skill now to my advantage. He tries to force me to gain some advantage from achieving these goals, to having this side of my character. What is the point of it all if you cannot profit from it, he assumes? He will never understand.

I wake and find myself on my knees in a fast flowing and freezing stream. I forced myself to my feet. How long had I been there?

With fury I checked my bearing on the compass again and forced myself onwards into the wind to make up lost time and cursed myself aloud for being foolish, my legs mere lumps of garish ice, numb and cumbersome. The map flapped annoying in my face and I cursed aloud my foolishness.

The luminous needle on the compass had become my only ally. I ignored the gravity of incline, up, down flat, none of it mattered, I knew the pace I had to keep to pass and persisted onwards, into the night.

I can only remember dawn breaking over the hills. The sun appeared quickly and lit the landscape. Wicked and cruel still testing me but at least showing its face. Dawn gave me renewed strength.

My friend came from behind me. A blurred memory as I write.

A tall, professional Marine I had got to know well over the course. Always stronger than me, he knew I was down.

Finished.

A hip flask appeared and I could have kissed him. The brown liquid warmed me and brought me back to life. He had stopped and risked failure for me.

"You're behind." I was told.

"Fucking move, the final check point is over the last ridge"

I know nothing from here, I just remember moving.

Some time later hands grabbed me and I was lifted. My huge bergan was un strapped and peeled away from my back, taking skin with it and I was suddenly floating.

I came to, groggy and in a fast moving vehicle and was sure I was still on the hills.

"Gotta get up" I shouted at the people around me.

"Keep going!" Rough hands pushed me back to the cold metal floor of the truck.

At five am the hospital was nice, warm and whatever they had pumped into me felt good.

I am warm, worn, and weary, yet still wandering in my mind thinking of my desk in less than twenty four hours.

My suit, my other tactics, how tired I know I will be and why I would not, could not discuss it with anyone. I thought of my family, my wife and kids. They were waiting at home.

"Have a good weekend?" They would inevitably ask as I shuffled into the office.

"Get up to much?"

I would excuse myself, why I was shuffling, would mumble something about being hung-over and tired.

Later that morning I was dropped back at the hills, stiff like an old man and beaten.

I was told my distance, by a battle hardened instructor who seemed pleased; forty two miles. And then time; eighteen hours fifty two minuets. And then weight; fifty five kilograms minus water and rifle.

I had made it.

"Bloody well done." He congratulated me as he squeezed my hand too tightly, still asserting authority..

Sitting under the modern spotlights of my office I think about my two different kinds of tactics. Two different kinds of lives.

One for the wage.

One to kill.

I allowed myself to smile. I had passed. One of few.

Halfway down the M4 another recruit whispered into his phone from the seat behind me.

Our drill conversation ceased as everyone in the minibus strained to hear his conversation. His head was bent into the seat in front and he struggled to keep his tone low.

The mans voice cracked as he sobbed through his words. His father had been in the Regiment for many years and recently retired. A well known and respected man, the weight of his own achievements carried heavily on his son's shoulders as he was expected to pass.

This man had not made the grade and he was telling his father that he would not get to serve. It was his second attempt. There would be no more chances. I could hear his fathers deep voice on the other end of the line but could not make out the words. I hoped they would be of reassurance, but I knew they were not. He had failed.

April

Weekend Warrior

**War is delightful to those who have no experience of it**

**Desiderius Eramus 1466**

"Well that little bump is over with then." Our officer commanding addressed us proudly from behind his lecturers' stand.

His small, round spectacles shone in the dim light and, as he threw his papers onto the wooden top in front of him, a cloud of dust rose up and covered his long, black hair. I assumed he was this confident in his barristers chambers a few hours before.

"Now the fun really begins-" He carried on

"-you've proved you can read a map and run over hills and bloody well done, buts that's all." We were warned. His failing Irish accent paused after the jump at the end of his speech.

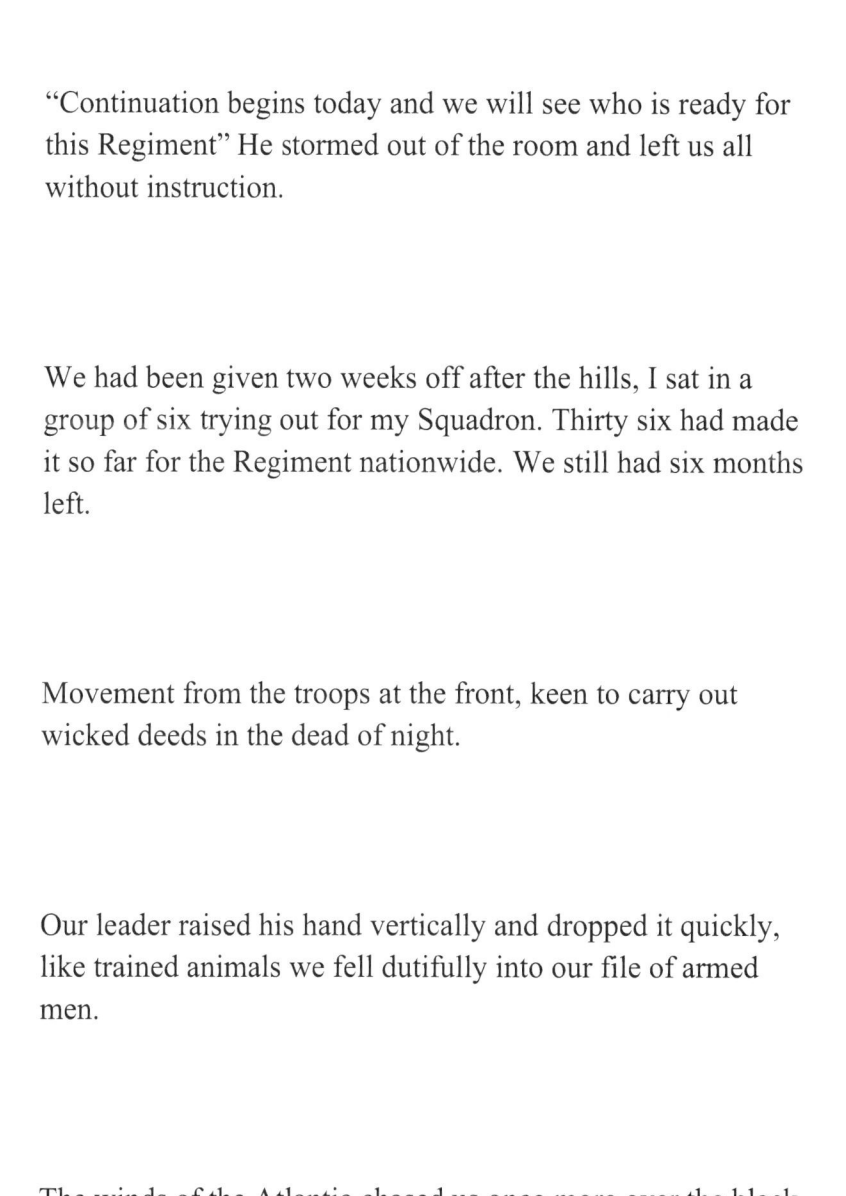

"Continuation begins today and we will see who is ready for this Regiment" He stormed out of the room and left us all without instruction.

We had been given two weeks off after the hills, I sat in a group of six trying out for my Squadron. Thirty six had made it so far for the Regiment nationwide. We still had six months left.

Movement from the troops at the front, keen to carry out wicked deeds in the dead of night.

Our leader raised his hand vertically and dropped it quickly, like trained animals we fell dutifully into our file of armed men.

The winds of the Atlantic chased us once more over the black ground. It accompanied me on a very different task, equally as difficult.

We patrolled, like shadows in the night. Drifting from cover to cover – fearful of any light or movement that might betray us.

We knew we would be attacked at some point, remaining watchful of our pretend deaths that lay ahead.

Shadows in the night threatened rapid violence as they watched us quietly, judging our every moves, seeing if the lessons had sunk in and we could act upon them in a real setting.

By weekend; learn how to be a warrior.

Near the end of the exercise one man decides not to go on. Fearful of moving over uneven ground in the dark, he risked injury, he said. Giving up now was a disgrace but he seemed frightened of failure so he brought it upon himself. He had been a regular soldier in the past, and now I think he had had enough of war. I don't remember his name now.

The patrol felt bitter towards him at stopping and losing a number, but all felt selfishly better at our own ability to carry on.

From a man made forestry block, muzzle flashes from within the tree line and the crack of small arms fire erupted, upsetting the tranquillity of the night.

Instinctively we dropped, into the wet grass, fearful of bullets that we knew did not exist. The training had made us believe – our minds were on a country at war and men some of us knew out there – soon it could be real and we had fought hard to be at the very front.

Our tiredness forgotten we spring forwards, moving in formation, winning our pretend battle, attacking like our forefathers did many times, but we were better, quicker, more accurate, we had learnt their lessons in battle and progressed through these lessons and with technology.

I had been given the patrol radio.

"Learn to use it by twenty three hundred hours." I had been told by a staff member at the drill hall before we set off.

It was the first time I had laid hands on the equipment and the task seemed impossible, for they knew I was a civilian learning everything. Another test.

Fortunately one of my patrol had been trained on the radio and he gave me a run down on way to the training area. I knew how to learn quickly.

"Alpha zero one this is zero one over." I whispered through gasping breaths into the mouth piece. I had to become part of the attack and remember my positioning and report the situation at the same time. I knew that an instructor within the tree line would be watching me through lumini infused night vision, judging my actions with scrutiny. There were so few of us left to watch you could get away with nothing now.

"Zero one this is alpha zero one send over." Came the crackled reply back in my ear set, I imagined the officer at the other end of the line sipping coffee in a warm Land Rover.

"Contact, contact." I whispered harshly, explosions were going off all around me and I struggled with remembering the correct military format.

"Await my sit rep over." I instructed briefly ending the exchange. I had to inform base of the contact but did not have the time to go into detail, the fight was still going on.

A member of my patrol next to me stood to run, he was a tall man, my friend from the hills and for a split second I admired his aggression and professionalism. He had done this for real before.

I moved with him changing a magazine on the run. Narrowly avoiding trees I opened up on the targets, a general purpose machine gun had been remotely triggered within the wood and, like swooping eagles, we were on it. Unsure of our next move after the fight we all fell silent staring at the smoking weapon.

We patrol away from the battle, our leader hissing orders through the darkness, angry that he has to use his voice.

"Alpha zero one this is zero one over." I whispered again into the mike.

"Keep that fucking voice down." I was told by the angry staff.

Heard only by me the voice came back, "Zero one send over."

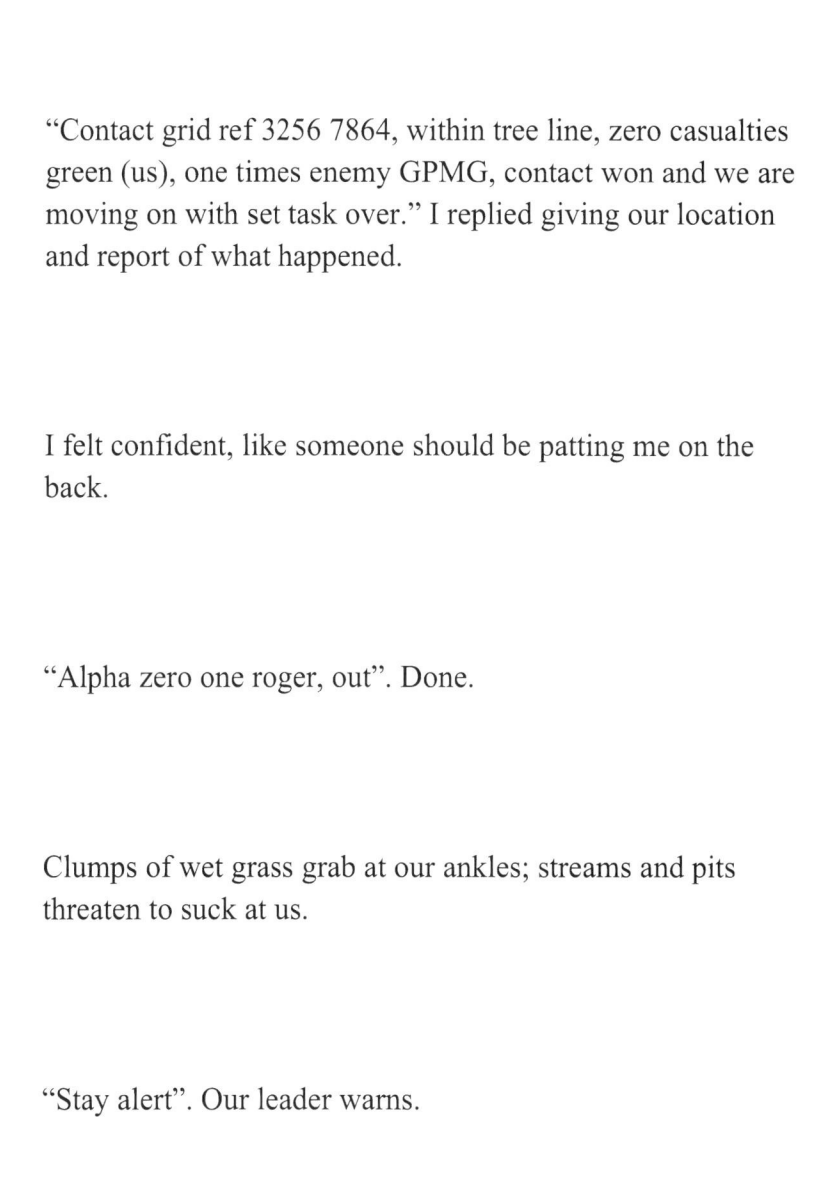

"Contact grid ref 3256 7864, within tree line, zero casualties green (us), one times enemy GPMG, contact won and we are moving on with set task over." I replied giving our location and report of what happened.

I felt confident, like someone should be patting me on the back.

"Alpha zero one roger, out". Done.

Clumps of wet grass grab at our ankles; streams and pits threaten to suck at us.

"Stay alert". Our leader warns.

The excellence of the staff is absolute in these situations. This is their stage.

On Sunday morning at four am I lay in a damp barn with no electrics. Adrenaline fading from my body, they make it seem so real. Experts in their craft. The wind whistles at the flimsy door, still trying to catch us.

I am weary. But it all felt very natural, just a job that I seem good at right away.

It was my thirtieth birthday.

Weekend over, test passed. Home.

Down to four men.

May


Camp


**The god of war hates those who hesitate.**


**Euripides 480BC**


"Don't do any sort of physical activity on that knee or carry any heavy weights on your back until the hospital can scan them. You've got cartilage damage and a trapped nerve, it could cause permanent damage" The doctor instructed me on Wednesday afternoon.

On Friday I set off on a two week Special Forces Selection camp.

For ten days, seventeen men including the boys from up North moved around the country at various military locations carrying out various degrees of tasks.

Although I knew them all reasonably well such confined space and close proximity open everyone's eyes.

The emotional pressure of what had been and what was required to pass tested all. I was the only non military person still left.

A very fit man lay next to me in a cold shell scrape somewhere in Aldershot at the dead of night. He was a bricklayer in his normal life and a serving member of a reserve unit in London and I liked to pal up with him. He was quiet and determined, I knew he had a young family.

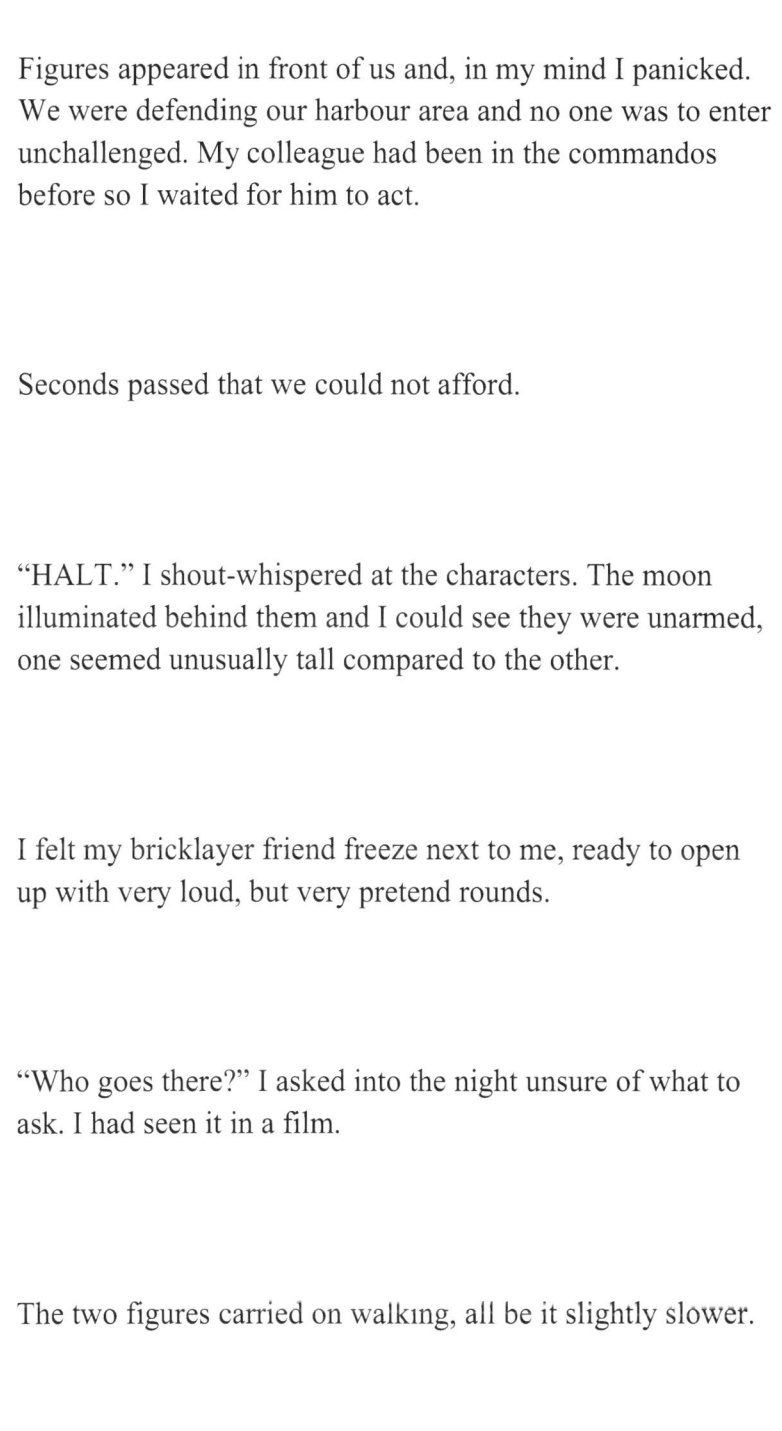

Figures appeared in front of us and, in my mind I panicked. We were defending our harbour area and no one was to enter unchallenged. My colleague had been in the commandos before so I waited for him to act.

Seconds passed that we could not afford.

"HALT." I shout-whispered at the characters. The moon illuminated behind them and I could see they were unarmed, one seemed unusually tall compared to the other.

I felt my bricklayer friend freeze next to me, ready to open up with very loud, but very pretend rounds.

"Who goes there?" I asked into the night unsure of what to ask. I had seen it in a film.

The two figures carried on walking, all be it slightly slower.

"HALT." I warned again. "Keep coming and we'll open up."

"Stand down that man." A male voice replied, not even trying to keep his voice down.

"I am staff sergeant Beresford and I am accompanying Brigadier Thrin from the local camp."

I paused. Surely this was not part of the programme. Another unusual test perhaps? I looked to the bricklayer for advice but he shrugged, happy to let me lead myself into potential disaster.

When in doubt, act as if training is real I decided. Aggression was the name of the game.

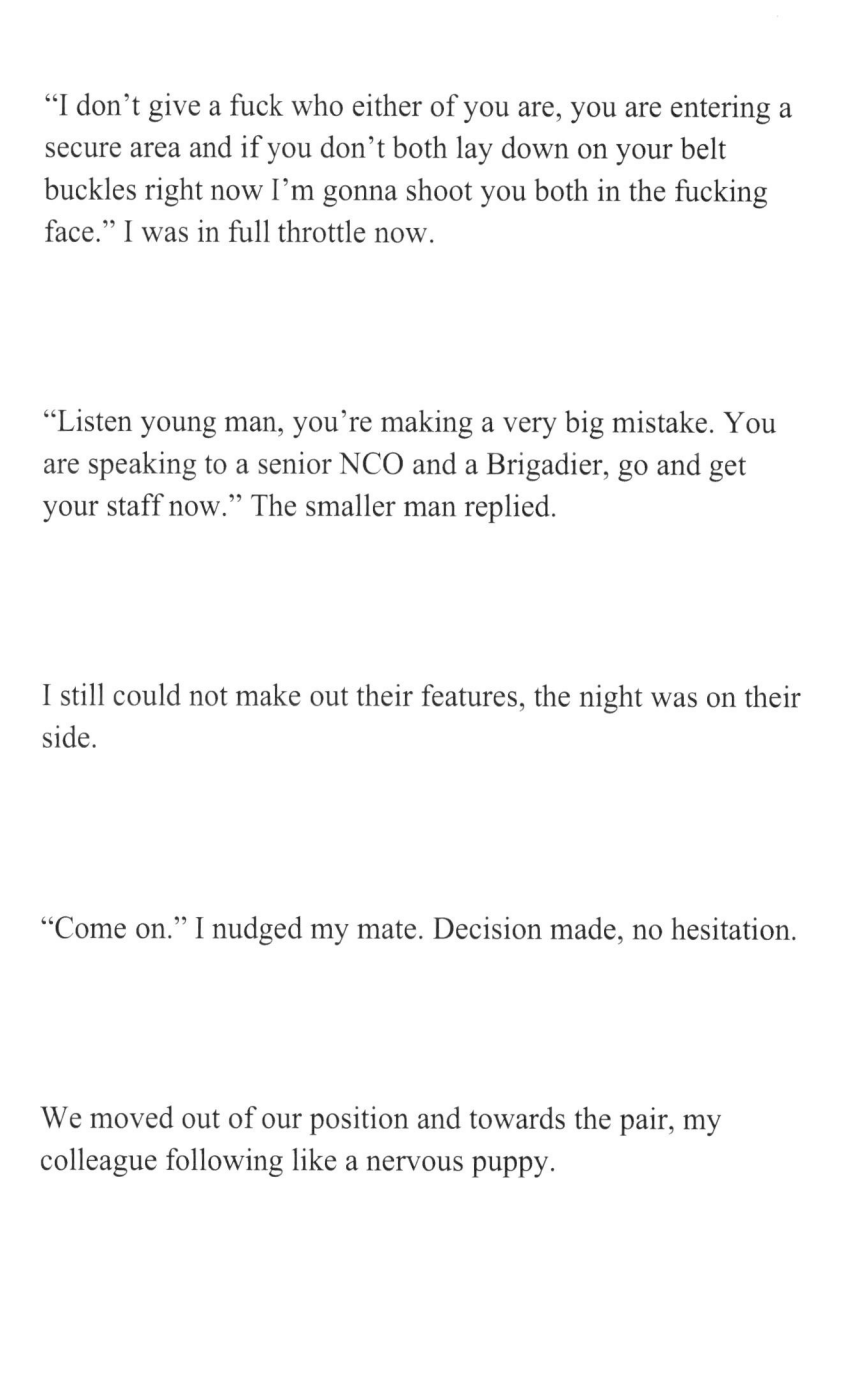

"I don't give a fuck who either of you are, you are entering a secure area and if you don't both lay down on your belt buckles right now I'm gonna shoot you both in the fucking face." I was in full throttle now.

"Listen young man, you're making a very big mistake. You are speaking to a senior NCO and a Brigadier, go and get your staff now." The smaller man replied.

I still could not make out their features, the night was on their side.

"Come on." I nudged my mate. Decision made, no hesitation.

We moved out of our position and towards the pair, my colleague following like a nervous puppy.

I gripped the larger of the two and forced him to his knees, he must have had a foot over me but I had the momentum and aggression. I could feel his shock.

"Get your fucking hands of him now." The smaller man warned, he moved towards me but bricklayer was faster and stronger. They were both down now in the dirt, faces flat.

A voice appeared behind asking what was happening. Finally our staff, had I passed this test?

Thirty minutes later I was being severely bollocked by a very angry Sergeant Major, my instructor and a very flustered Brigadier stood by under the light of a red torch beam.

What they had said was true, it was the first time reserve special forces had used the training area and the Brigadier wanted to surprise us at night and "inspect our lines". A stupid move but he owned the place after all. He regretted it I am sure.

As the pair stormed off into the night our staff member came over to me, as the entire camp listened quietly.

He was a wiry, bald man who had a fearsome reputation as an amateur boxer, He was well known in the Regiment for being nasty, everyone hated him.

I had already mentally packed my bags home.

He put his face right in mine and I felt the tickle of his moustache in the night. His dark eyes flickered back and forth as I felt his breath against my face.

"Well done." He finally said quietly. Then left to go back to his basher.

It was two am.

"Put it away now." A member of the training team was in my face again, it was still night and I had been awake for twenty seven hours.

"What you fucking waiting for?" Barely a hair between our faces.

I tried to stuff my poncho into the top pouch of my bergan, my hands shaking with cold and exhaustion, as fast as I could but he was relentless.

"You're fucking useless." He accused as I struggled with the zip.

At all these testing times I made myself realise it was all a game, a test of my sanity, self control.

The small group made it way to the ranges as dawn broke, ahead of us lay a hundred miles of fine English country side, we were there to destroy the first five hundred yards of it.

Weapons from every corner of the earth were produced, stripped, discussed, explained, analysed and fired over the next ten hours. It was every small boy and grown soldiers dream. One of the same.

I stole another brief moment to myself, little moments I had where I could reflect. They were very important, I told myself again it was not real.

I lay, still at the firing point in the prone position, my weapon of choice still pointed down the range in menace. I had emptied my magazine and could still feel the heat from the muzzle, a paper figure of a running man riddled with holes stood two hundred yards away. The grimace of aggression still on his helmeted face although he was well and truly dead.

I waited for the other men to finish firing as I watched a lumbering beetle, stumble and fall over an empty shell that sat hot next to me on the ground. I wondered how many more like him were down at the wrong end of the range "getting the bad news" as the instructors would say. It all became clear then. Death would be too easy in such situations.

The air of excitement with the other men in the group at the vast range of weaponry was electric that day. They had dreamed of this moment, most of them soldiers since their teens. I tried to share their enthusiasm, pretended to even, but it just was not there.

I suppose I kept thinking about what these things of metal were designed for. Not paper.

"GAS GAS GAS" Our staff shouted with a muffled voice.

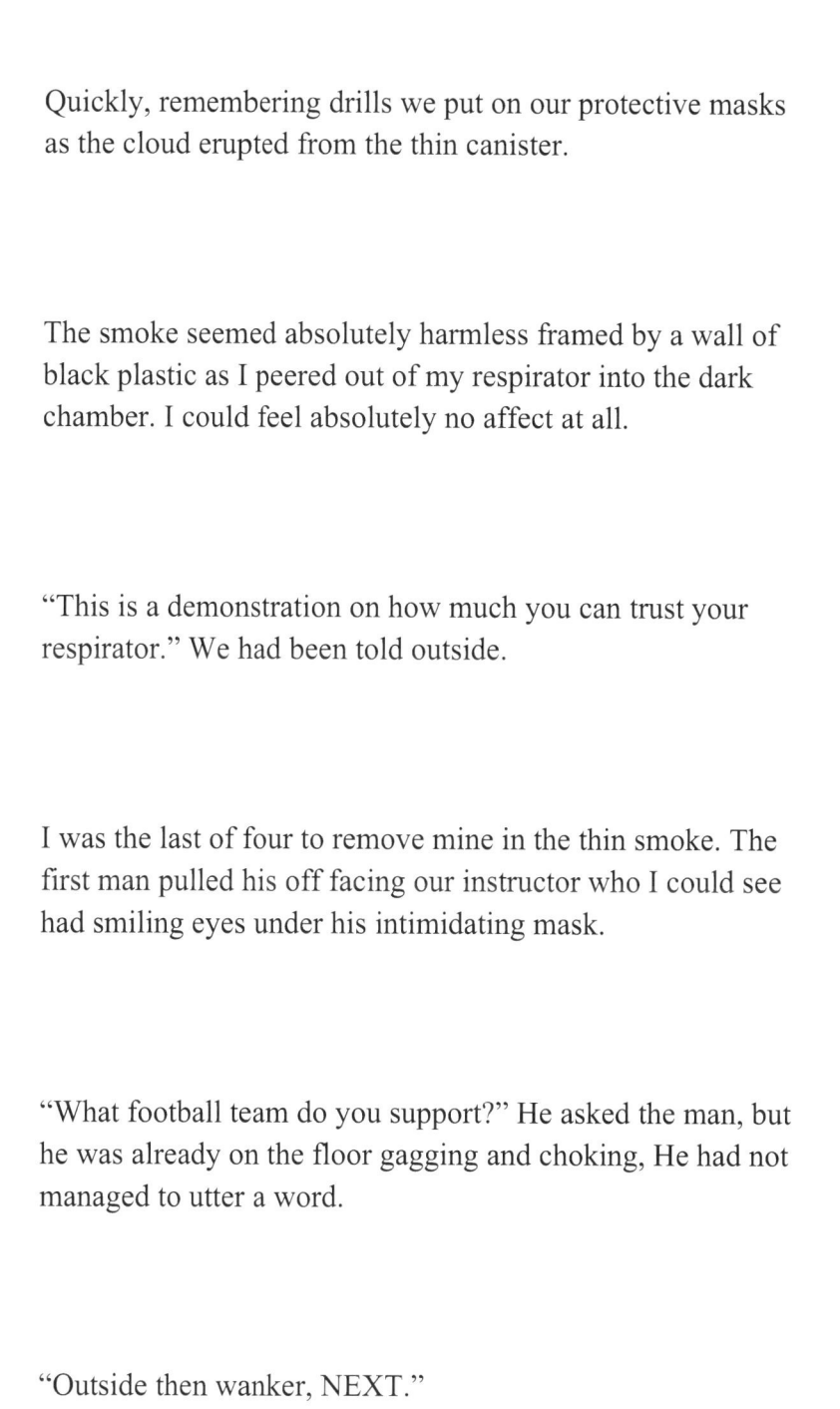

Quickly, remembering drills we put on our protective masks as the cloud erupted from the thin canister.

The smoke seemed absolutely harmless framed by a wall of black plastic as I peered out of my respirator into the dark chamber. I could feel absolutely no affect at all.

"This is a demonstration on how much you can trust your respirator." We had been told outside.

I was the last of four to remove mine in the thin smoke. The first man pulled his off facing our instructor who I could see had smiling eyes under his intimidating mask.

"What football team do you support?" He asked the man, but he was already on the floor gagging and choking, He had not managed to utter a word.

"Outside then wanker, NEXT."

The man threw himself at the door and rushed out into the wind.

The next victim managed to state his surname but again hit the floor and was ushered out, choking.

The third not much better. Part of me wondered if it could be that bad.

Finally in the dark chamber stood myself and my staff. My thick chemical, biological, radiological and nuclear camouflaged suit bore my name and number so he knew who I was despite my famous disguise.

"Right then, take your mask off" I was ordered.

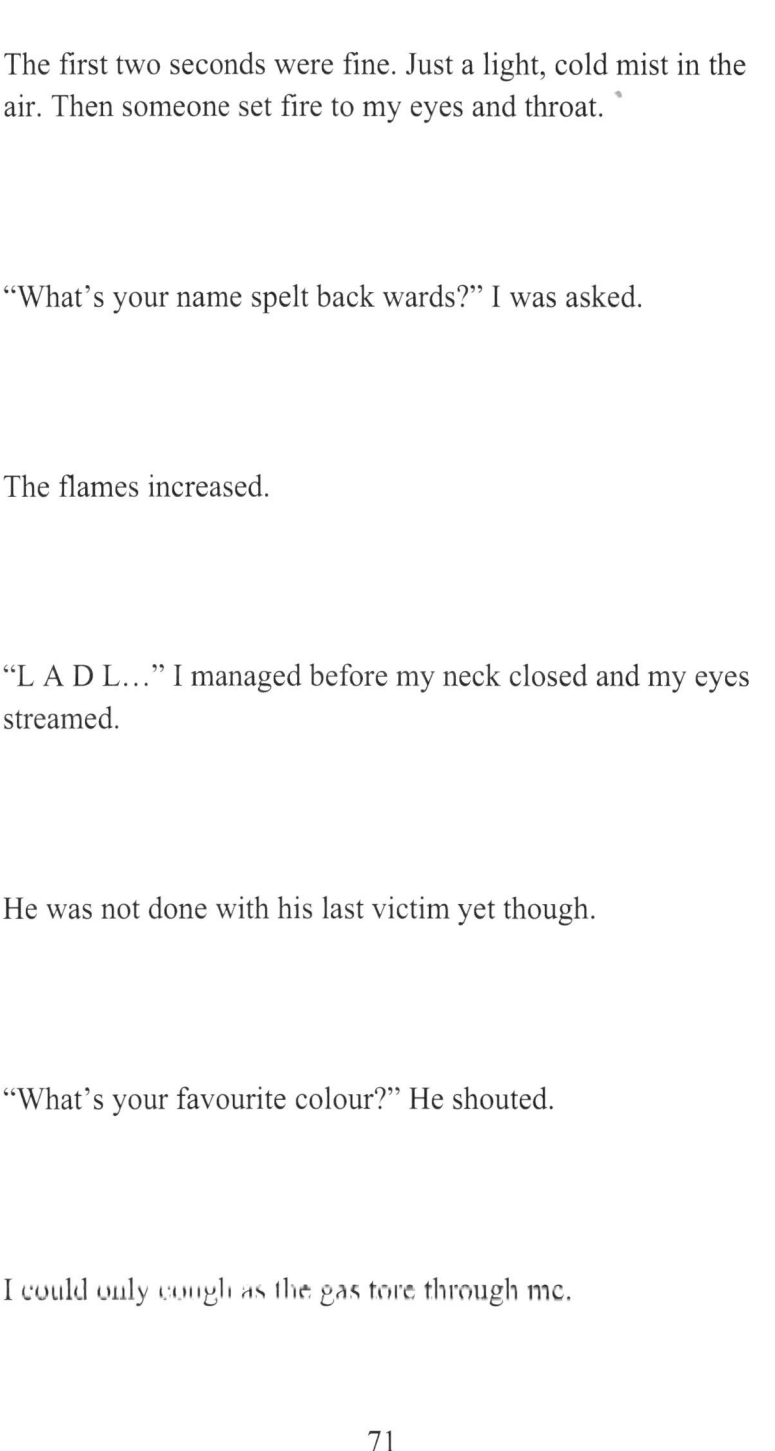

The first two seconds were fine. Just a light, cold mist in the air. Then someone set fire to my eyes and throat.

"What's your name spelt back wards?" I was asked.

The flames increased.

"L A D L…" I managed before my neck closed and my eyes streamed.

He was not done with his last victim yet though.

"What's your favourite colour?" He shouted.

I could only cough as the gas tore through me.

"Go on then, fuck off."

I raced out into the wind not daring to touch my burning face. The gas affects moisture and to touch your eyes would only add to the suffering.

Lesson learned, trust your respirator.

The next five days were made of written tests, lessons and physical training, test on medical and combat first aid, chemical, nuclear, patrol skills, section attacks, signalling, skill at arms, advanced geographical study, language, weapon handling on several terminals, information on other militaries and their weaponry and vehicles, un armed combat, obstacle crossing, river crossing, patrol tactics, advanced reconnaissance, photography, range finding, observation, hide building , camouflage and concealment, section attacks, patrol formations, hand signals, personal radio operation, chemical attack drills, fire and manoeuvre, the principles and practices of marksmanship, patrol defence, harbour area defence, distance calculation, and surprisingly, some light marching just to remind us we were soldiers.

Every thing was taught in detail and tested fully, a culmination of months of hard work condensed into a few days testing with may more to comeback at our reserve centre's, should we find success.

The days were full and long. Five am starts and eleven pm finished. Food was always quick and the physicality of the course never relented.

A few faces quietly disappeared and were not discussed as they fell at the tests. Their kit packed up and gone. We never saw them go. It was arranged by the staff like that.

A hard days exercise and lessons would be followed by a night of studying for a six am exam. Everyone of them had to be passed first time. No exceptions.

We moved around the country but the pressure remained.

You would not believe what you can fit into twenty four hours.

May

Escape, Evasion, Interrogation

**Wars may be fought with weapons, but they are won by men.**

**General George Patton Jr**

Three of us remained from the squadron I was trying to join. A large ex commando who stood six feet seven inches tall, by profession he was an arbitress and had a degree from a good university, he also had a long criminal record for football hooliganism, a truly conflicting character.

He had given up his home, fiancée and good job in pursuit of the Regiment.

The next man was an ex lancer from the West Country. His wife had left him just before camp and he shrugged at the mention of it. He like to run "at least five triathlons a year." He was quick and quiet. They both fitted in.

My tall, commando friend and I swapped our thick great coats away from the prying eyes of the staff. I had been given one much too big and his, too small. Under them I wore an issued polyester T – shirt, combat trousers with no belt, boots with no laces and carried only a hand drawn map covering about twenty miles of countryside. I looked like a cartoon tramp.

We set off at one hour intervals, I was second to leave, alone into the dusk.

Capture was inevitable but the time between departure and capture was scrutinised.

Two hours later night had fallen and I screwed myself into a bramble bush watching a man standing openly in a middle of a road. His movements were careful and he watched like a hawk.

I remembered my lesson from my teens and did not move until I had made the decision to expose myself, pleased that he had not seen me and the choice was mine.

He rushed towards in full acting mode.

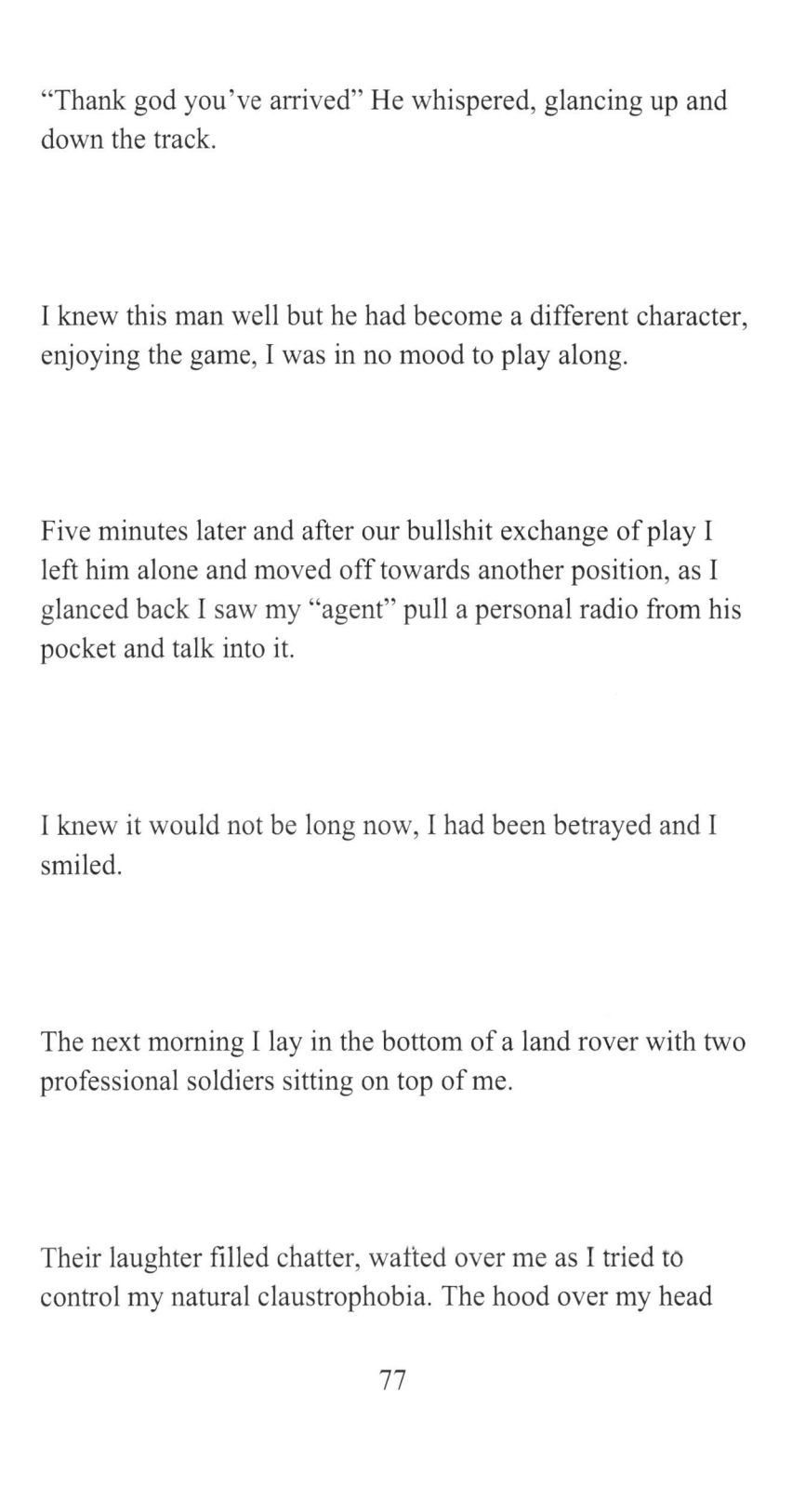

"Thank god you've arrived" He whispered, glancing up and down the track.

I knew this man well but he had become a different character, enjoying the game, I was in no mood to play along.

Five minutes later and after our bullshit exchange of play I left him alone and moved off towards another position, as I glanced back I saw my "agent" pull a personal radio from his pocket and talk into it.

I knew it would not be long now, I had been betrayed and I smiled.

The next morning I lay in the bottom of a land rover with two professional soldiers sitting on top of me.

Their laughter filled chatter, wafted over me as I tried to control my natural claustrophobia. The hood over my head restricted my breathing and the weight of them squeezed my chest flat against the steel. It would be over soon.

I find myself shivering in an empty room. A door must be open as my tiredness and hunger make the cold much worse. My arms raised high above my head and my legs spread, away from the wall. The hood takes any vision, guess work is all I can go on.

We wondered at the routine before hand, had read about it from previous members but it always changes to keep recruits on their toes.

Finally I am dragged away from the wall and kicked harshly in the back of my legs, the movement is welcome.

I am pushed down and the hood pulled from my head, fluorescent lights pierce my vision and I blink, trying desperately to focus to gain some advantage on my surroundings.

I sigh loudly, encouraging myself to stay alert, don't be tricked.

A man questions me for half an hour, prying, twisting and turning with his questions, trying to trick me into a wrong answer. He threatens violence, promises food and warmth and finally sends me away, disgusted at my resilience.

The hood goes back on and the wall reapers in front of me, another kick and I am back in the cold, piercing pain.

Two women laugh at me as I stand before them naked. Stripped of all possessions and self-worth. I am cold and shivering fiercely. They mock me, "what the fuck am I doing here?" They tease.

One walks behind me a squeezes my behind and the other flicks my manhood with the edge of her boots as she sits on the desk. Head bent down, playing the part of the captive, I slip briefly as I laugh with them, then instantly cover it with a cough. Its just a game, I tell myself.

They get nothing from me either, I win that round.

I haven't eaten in over twenty four hours and I weaken against the wall. My legs wobble and I slip, a kick to my legs wakens me and I stand again, hoping that I did not mutter a word as I fell away.

The routine drags on and on, different people, with different questions but the wall, the hood and the cold remain.

Hours later I am taken outside and the hood removed, a familiar face is there and hands me a milky coffee, thick with sugar. I did not say anything, I have passed the exercise with a good score. My female friends in laughter awarded me the highest.

Later I find myself alone in a minibus as we await the other recruits to come out and be told if they have succeeded. I take the solitude of the moment to cry. It took everything I had.

May

Parade

**How fortunate for leaders that men do not think.**

**Adolf Hitler**

"Today is a big day-" We were told by an instructor, this staff member was slightly built but ruthless. A top marathon runner he weighed little but was fiercely strong and determined. Younger than me but an expert in his craft, I liked him.

Every man sitting on their beds sat up right, an immediate air of tension gripped the room as we thought news was pending. Who had passed?

"-not for you wankers, but for some young men and women who are passing out today from this camp to join their regiments." Our shoulders slumped, another cruel trick.

"Don't look sorry for yourselves." The laughing instructor went on, "If you're good boys and girls we'll go and let you watch them pass out on parade in front of their families."

No one still knew who had passed tactical questioning or even camp. They dragged it out to plague our minds.

Three hours later we stood just behind a large stand filled with families of all ages, in the largest military training centre in the South.

A few of us had washed but many had not found the energy, we had all done what we could do, it was out of our hands now, home was just around the corner.

The huge parade square in front of us was stagnant with immovable young men and women. Polished and perfect they stood erect, younger than us, a solid block of professionalism.

Orders were barked and the band played on throughout, the crowd cheered and women cried. The best of them were given awards by my Brigadier friend and the applause was genuine from their proud loved ones.

We remained hidden in the shadows watching, my fellow recruits and instructors had seen it all before but, it dawned on me this was the first I had ever seen of the "real" army. I had missed this stage and gone straight into the elite. It did not seem fair somehow as I admired them.

A man appeared around the corner from us and approached, naturally the recruits shied away but our instructor stood firm.

The man was heavy in the belly and grey at the top but he walked with the air of self confidence of a military man.

Quietly he spoke with our instructor never taking his eyes of the square.

"That's my grandson-" I heard him say gesturing towards the middle.

"-REME he's off to, better than the bloody infantry."

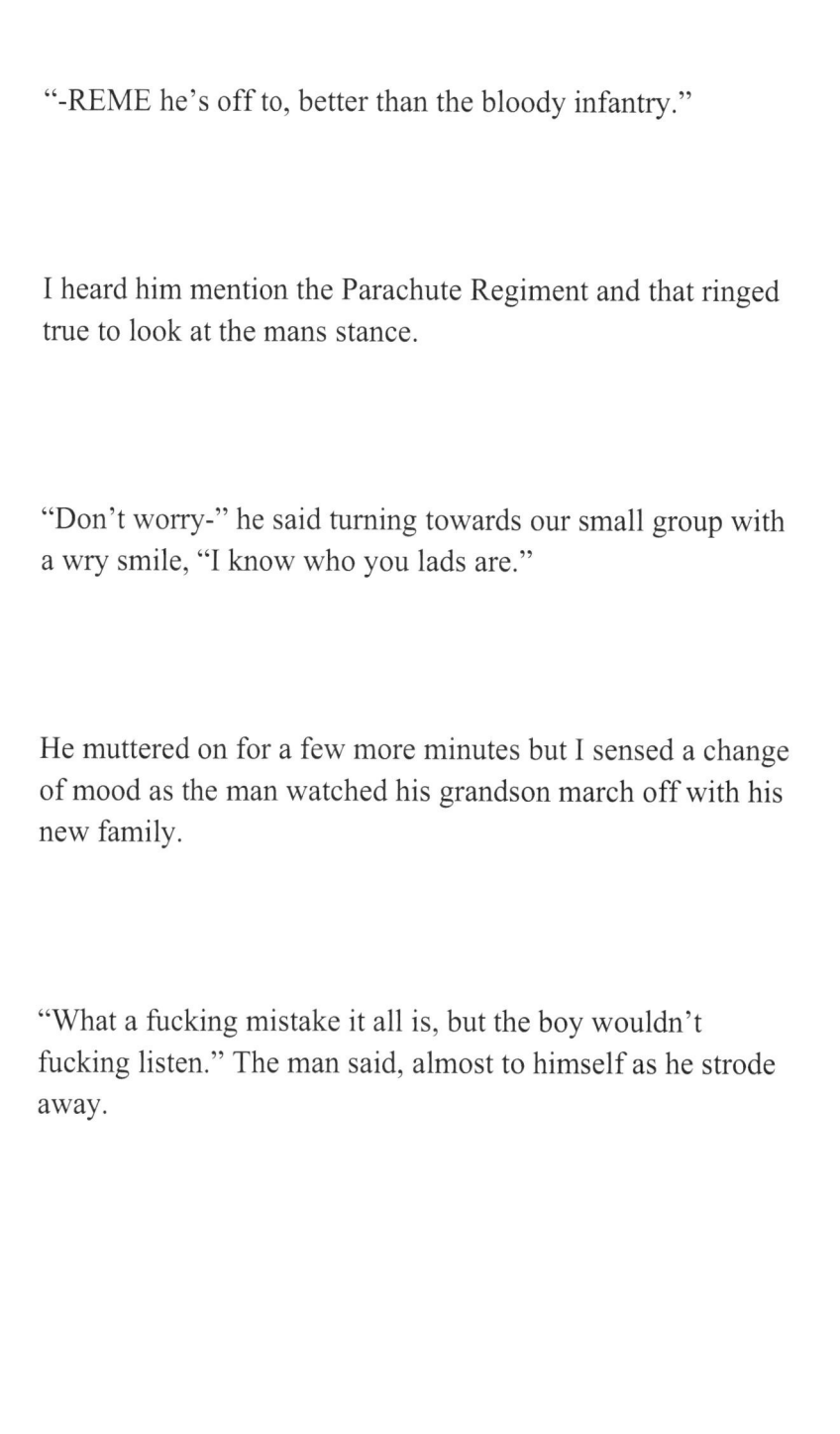

I heard him mention the Parachute Regiment and that ringed true to look at the mans stance.

"Don't worry-" he said turning towards our small group with a wry smile, "I know who you lads are."

He muttered on for a few more minutes but I sensed a change of mood as the man watched his grandson march off with his new family.

"What a fucking mistake it all is, but the boy wouldn't fucking listen." The man said, almost to himself as he strode away.

August

Throwing Oneself from a Moving Aircraft

**As men, we are all equals in the presence of death.**

**Publilius Syrus 100BC**

What regular paratroopers learn in three wakes for basic jumps we had to learn in a very long night after the office.

My tall, commando friend and I remained. A lonely, very different pair in physical and moral form.

Our Lancer had not made the grade with the interrogators as his aggression got the better of him and tiredness and hunger made him lash out at a threat in one of the rooms. He was at home while we took off on a bright summer morning in a small aircraft over Wiltshire. None of us had cared to say goodbye after camp.

My colleague had jumped before, I had not. It was the final test of character.

The door was pulled to one side as the aircraft reached the optimum height and our drills from the night before kicked in. My tiredness forgotten as the wind stuck me and the ground below became clear.

Hand signals were shared and my friend went first, his large body flew through the open door, then I did not hesitate.

Seconds later I lay on the wet grass staring up, the aircraft was landing a few hundred yards away and my adrenaline fading.

I had not enjoyed it. It hurt and the fear remained but I had done it. I lit a cigarette as I traipsed back to the runway.

Many times that day we took off as a small group and threw ourselves into the clear air. It became more enjoyable as the day drew on and the expectation ceased from the staff.

As dusk fell I stood in full kit and rifle for the final jump.

The large, military aircraft lumbered out of a hanger and the back, dropped with a clang. So cumbersome on the ground but free and nimble in the sky.

I shuffled into the dark exterior and, finally the engines burst as we elevated above the ground.

As the back dropped again the aircraft shook, caught in the air. We threw ourselves out of the gaping back and, almost instantly my parachute jolted me back.

Floating, checking, Always checking. Alert

The dark ground rushed up to meet me for the final time.

Late on Sunday I was at home with my wife. The children were in bed. The contrast in my life once more so obvious. I went outside for a cigarette and looked up from our small garden at the night sky. I felt some ownership to it now.

October

The Prize

**There's a lot to be said for self-delusionment when it comes to matters of the heart.**

**Diane Frolov**

" Bloody well done mate, welcome to the family. You were a fucking big surprise to be honest but you impressed most of the way. Word of advice though, keep you're trap shut, no one really cares anyway and they certainly will never understand."

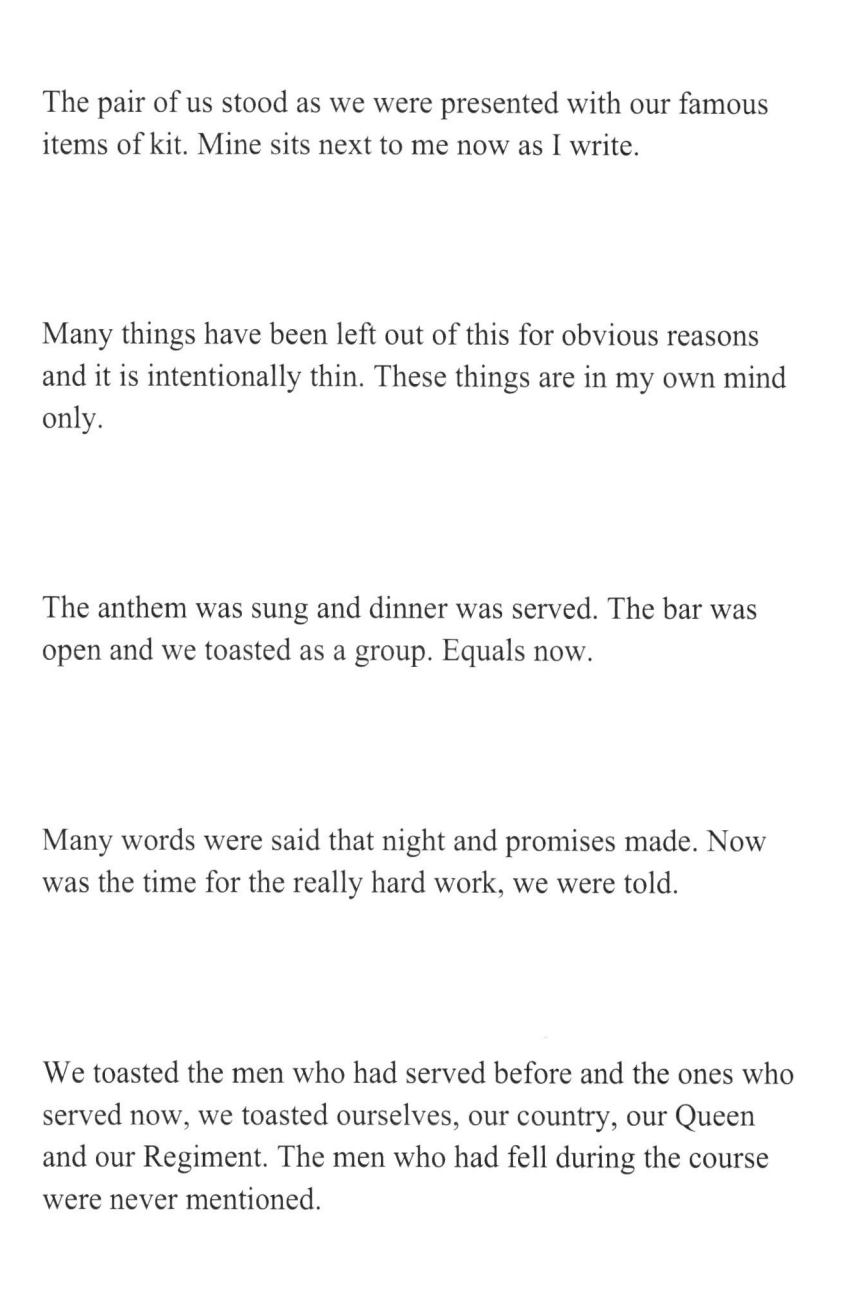

The pair of us stood as we were presented with our famous items of kit. Mine sits next to me now as I write.

Many things have been left out of this for obvious reasons and it is intentionally thin. These things are in my own mind only.

The anthem was sung and dinner was served. The bar was open and we toasted as a group. Equals now.

Many words were said that night and promises made. Now was the time for the really hard work, we were told.

We toasted the men who had served before and the ones who served now, we toasted ourselves, our country, our Queen and our Regiment. The men who had fell during the course were never mentioned.

Aggression spilled over that night, fuelled by alcohol as men fought and then laughed. A true boys club, but for dangerous, very different men.

I cycled home in the early hours of the morning, swaying as I went. My beret and belt in my pockets and happy.

I was weary but proud. My mind was still made up, I had my secret from my new family.

January

Home time

**We not only look at things from different points of view, but with different eyes; we do not care to find them alike.**

**Pascal**

My corporal told me things I already knew. There would be no going back.

I was giving up something great, it was great to him but I had something better, I thought.

My colleague who passed with me knew my decision and he was visibly shocked but did not care, he had already immersed himself fully and set about on his own path.

As I stood to leave, the grey haired man shook my hand firmly.

"Thanks for your time-" he said without a smile. Any emotion he had was gone.

I turned to leave and, with one hand on the door he spoke one last time, "Remember, it's not a game, it never was and if you wanted a round of applause you should have joined the fucking circus!"

The End

Printed in Great Britain
by Amazon